"In this fully mature first book, Sherry Cook Stanforth braids together place, family, and music in imagery that ranges from homey as 'hominy and banjos' to taut as a dulcimer's string. *Drone String* re-members the familial past, and imagines how, through the integrative power of tradition and memory, that past is part of now, insistent and intact. Vivid portraits and telling anecdotes remind us that all our lives are worthy, full of stories and meaning. A professor-musician, and part of a family band for decades, Stanforth has an ear for how people really sound, and for how poetry dances language into song."

~Dick Hague, author of *Where Drunk Men Go*

Bottom Dog Press

Drone String

Poems

Sherry Cook Stanforth

Appalachian Writing Series
Bottom Dog Press
Huron, Ohio

Credits
General Editor: Larry Smith
Cover Design: Susanna Sharp-Schwacke
Cover Photo Art: Tim Creamer
(Photo from Fraley Festival of Traditional Music,
Carter Caves State Resort Park.
Olive Hill, Kentucky. September 2014.)
Author photo: inside book: David Stanforth,
back cover: Stacy Rogers

Acknowledgments

Thank you to my beloved family members and friends for encouraging me during the writing of *Drone String*. Among these folks, none were more gracious with their time and reflective energy than my grandmother, Mary Curlis, my daughter, Corinne Stanforth, and my friends, Pauletta Hansel, Dick Hague and Michael Moran.

Finally, thank you to my parents, Nan and Jim Cook, who brought me into this world and then tucked me inside a circle of traditional music. I hope that these poems bring honor to the people and home places that continue to tune my sense of family experience and imagination.

Further Acknowledgments on page 87.

Contents

III. Who'll Rock the Cradle When I'm Gone?

For Grandma Mary

Sherry Cook (Stanforth), Vesta Vandora Dyer (Wade), John Caleb
Wade, Mary B. Wade (Curlis), James Allan Cook
Photograph taken in Madisonville, Tennessee, 1967.

Vesta Vandora (Dyer) Wade (1887-1975)
Photo taken by Pamela Janice, year unknown.

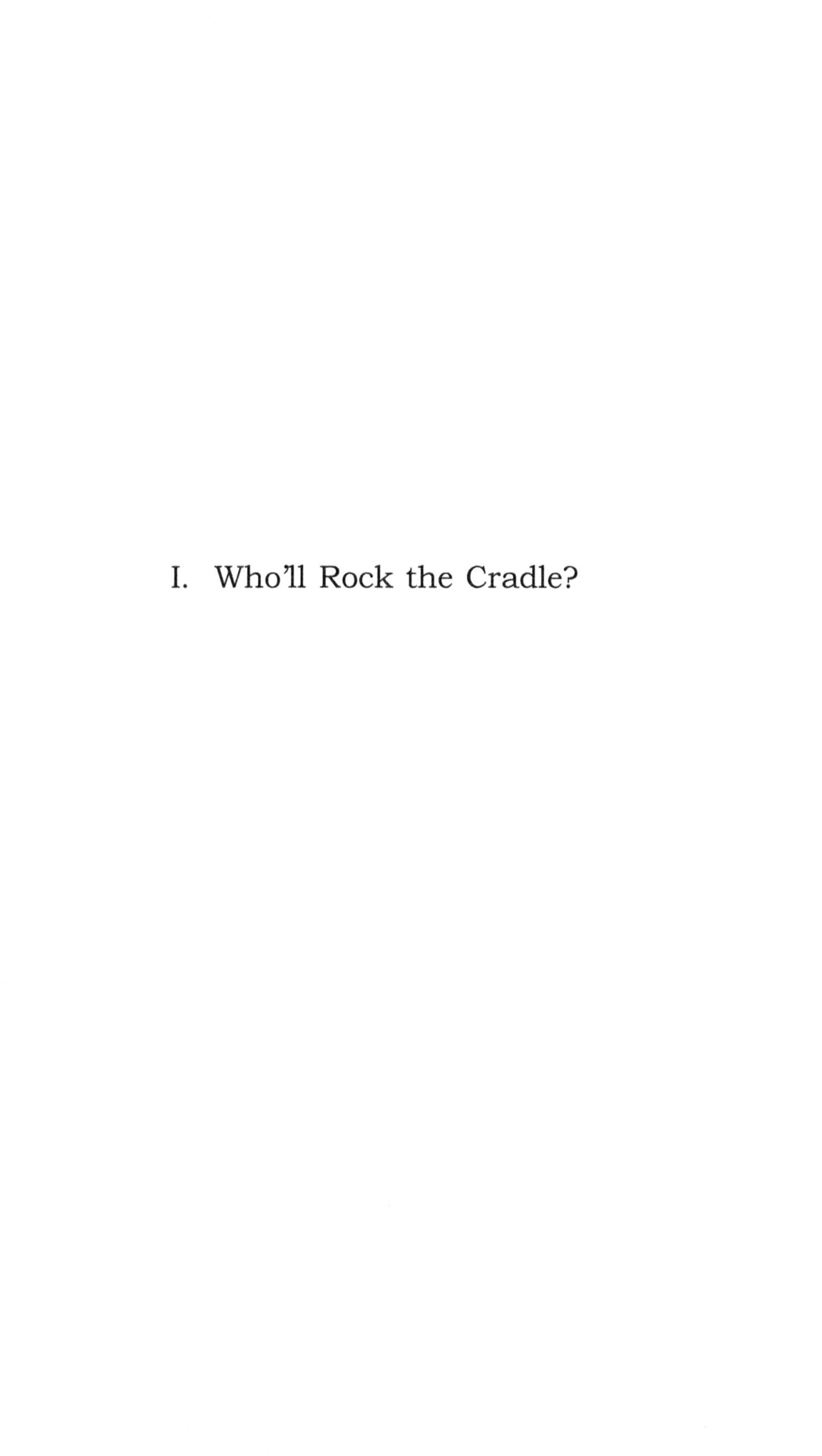

I. Who'll Rock the Cradle?

Woman, Creek Walking

Not bone but the absence
of bone—a socket stops
her and she leans low

over lichen spotted stones,
just to be sure. She fishes up
wedges of skull rippled gray

by water's slick tongue, studies
the hairline cracks spun along
a grooved nasal cavity while

her hounds track April's wet
edges, racing through chickweed
patches, then sniffing the oddity

gripped in her hand. Who stood
in this spot where she now stands
hungering for pinto beans left

bubbling in a crock on her kitchen
counter? *Go down to the water—
leave your troubles behind.* Stone-

hopping long stretches of creek,
she carries away what she finds—
though when experts come,

she grieves the splitting moment
she spent walking without thought,
then stopping over quiet bones.

Great-Grandma's Crow Lament

Talk about bad signs—one time
a crow flew in the breezeway door
right into the kitchen. Quick,
I slammed down a skillet still
hot in my hand. That bird bled
out a rain puddle, black glass eyes
chilling me to the bone a hundred
nights after. I kneeled down to Jesus,
cleaned that shadow the minute
it took to my threshold. No matter—
by season's end your Papaw was dead
and me alone with things falling down
around my head, save two babies still
sleeping in the cradle. Years I tried
keeping us tied together—told how
that man could sing, could hew us a table
out of stone hard ash, how he downed
a wildcat in one shot up there on the ridge
in the fallen dark. Hear me good, girl:
set your mind to lose whatever you got
in this world, 'cause nothing steals back time
or keeps a man in place once he's called—
not even a sharp-eyed woman quickened
by cast iron, hell-bent on barring the door.

Indulgence

Bored, I sat on the breezeway stoop
playing with an old glass salt shaker—
stuck out my tongue like a cow
or corn snake, sprinkling grains
until my spit trickled. Grandma threw
open the screen door, scolding "Girl,
you're surely gonna strangle on that.
Now give it here." I learned then
that too much of a good thing
could bind you up like white rice—
or corrode your insides yellow
with poison. Too many beers
or boys could spawn stories over
four counties. You got to be salt
of the earth by living close to dirt,
hoeing fields and weeding pole
bean rows in Georgia heat.

I was taken on down to the garden
and handed a weed sack. "We never
wanted much," she said, stooping
to point out crabgrass, telling how
they made ends meet on warmed
over soup and beans, beans, beans.
She'd say, "We got by" and then
let fly some memory of biting back
anger or that urge to give up
things for lost. "Gotta mend
tears, tend the fields, make do
shivering in the cold back room
or settling the junked edges
of some next home town."
Her one endless extra
was talk—cheap only
to those who'd never
tasted it in season.

Shopes' Field

Passing through Jellico's bent-up
I-75 stretches, Grandma slaps
the wheel and raises her voice
over the radio, claiming the North
for herself, rolling eyes at my love
for hominy and banjos, tossing good
old Dixie right under the bus—
Only good path is the one
leading straight outta here.

I want to argue back, but know
I'd better hush my mouth since
the South is where she grew
that bitter story of pulling up
yams in Shopes' field, paying
back old favors for her mother—
the use of a combine in fall,
extra milk in a pinch, the rent
let slide when Grandpa was sick.
No words to spit about
good Christians who helped
in hard Depression times.

The school bus flew past where
she worked the knotted clumps,
filling up her sack. Kids smacked
the windows, calling out on their way
to see *Gone With the Wind*. She stood
then, chucking yams right in their dust.
If staying home was what the South
was all about, then soon enough
she would yank
up everything
by the roots,
not give
a damn—

what ever it took
to make her own way.

What Mary B. Remembered

One time I thought I'd get wise
and stick them dirty pans
in the oven during company,
but Mother found them out
all right and made me wash
every dish in that kitchen.
I was up into the wee hours—
never did that again I tell you.
Out the back field every May
hoeing that baked garden till
we nearly blistered raw to bone.
Never any time to rest or play—
we either dug or was laying by.
She wouldn't give for us to sit
on any work *ever* so we ironed
hand towels and pillow cases.
I swore I'd *never* iron a linen
long as I lived and breathed—
you can bet to this day I will buy
permanent press or *nothing.*
Garden's not my thing either.
Mrs. Maddox's tomatoes
do me just fine in summer
so don't tell me about the South,
honey girl, cause I'm here to tell
you we was sweatin' it out
all those years and nothing's
what it's cracked up to be—
break your back, *that's* what.

App, Too

Don't ask me why I didn't grow up in a ram-shackle shack with red dirt floors and a front porch washing machine, and why my teeth are so shiny and straight from Coke in a baby bottle. My white fangs gleam, they are cut from Blue Ridge granite and they can scrape you down to bare bone with academically pruned, heteroglossic, hegemony-sensitive, specialized inter-disciplinary discourse peppered with Appalachian spice. Go ahead and roll your eyes at the way I wrap my mountain identity around me like a crazy quilt forged stitch by stitch by some withered up sooth-saying holler witch. My twang too educated for you? And my education just doesn't jive at all with your portrait of Rocky Top You'll Always Be a barefoot pregnant hilljack daughter, daddy don't work, watch them verbs, corn-fed Mama got fat on Twinkies, porch twanging hoe-down in a tattered skirt princess? Well, my daddy worked hard when he was ten—his shadow stretched across the lines of white pine he cut down with his great-granddaddy to feed a table full of kin. Where you been? Thirteen years of night school later, he took an engineering degree all for curly-headed me, his darling barefoot baby. My cow-milking, egg-snatching, chicken-chopping mama can pluck you like a drone string on a dulcimer and tune your judgment until it snaps in two like aging catgut. I'll sing you down. I'll spin a ballad around you so tight you can't breathe your next question about my PhD, my tax bracket, my way with turning words into a philosophical mind racquet to beat away your death grip on my spirit. I am red dirt flecked with mica in your eye. I'm the Cherokee mountain white girl guilt hope shooting down the Cherohala Skyway to surprise your low-slag stripped-down-to-bedrock expectations of the folks. I will teach and teach and reach for your shadow. I'll swallow it whole, and then I'll eat up all your dirt and grow kudzu green until everything you refuse to see is covered, made gone.

Tree Hugger

The chainsaw's buzz
        woke me
Saturday's gray grain fading—
I'd slept way too long again, went

to find my father standing in the yard,
        bent on his task.
"What?" I asked, saw plum branches
lopped into a lacy white circle.

Those arms had held my best secrets—
        sitting inside,
I'd dreamed of crushes and escape. When
he leaned in to chop again, I shrieked "No!"

and he shot me a look, shook his head.
        My tree had to go
if I wanted a new garage. I didn't.
I snapped *Who gives a damn* about pouring

footers or storing a stupid truck and tools.
        Plum blooms waved—maybe
at me, first planted against my ruined tree, then
tearing off to the house to hide from his long reach.

Stick to the Path

No, no, no, no, no
      Do not climb the sweet gum—
you know that's dangerous.
      Stay away
from the creek—it is noxious, nasty.
      God, don't touch that
bug, that flower. Who knows
            if it's poisonous?
      Don't look at the sun unless
you want to scar your retina.
      Don't walk in the hot night
under a gibbous moon
            or you'll be ravaged.
      And if you sing
nonsense songs on the swing
to your imaginary friend
who made you—
      well, people will say
            you're off your rocker.
No, no, no, no, no—
      close the gates and follow
these instructions to the letter.
      Don't you go
            losing your head, girl.

Bloody Mary

Once she shuts the door, the giggling
stops. Lock clicks, then a big "shhh"
breathing down to calm. AquaNet
and cinnamon gum, a whiff of vodka

quick slung at midnight and chased
by Cherry Coke. Shoulder to shoulder
we stand in the vanity's glow, preparing
for the terrible coming. "Do not wake

my mother," she warns. Lights out,
candle lit, she tells about the scarred
face running with blood and we squeeze
hands, dig in fingernails when she begins

the count. "Bloody Mary one. Bloody Mary
two." Pressed in the corner, I hear panting
inside the words, feel heat rising at my
core. Numbers mount and fog my brain.

I imagine horror unleashed, mashing
us all into goo. Only a scream away,
her mother rattles the door: "Girls,
stop this nonsense now," then slippers

snap along the night-smudged hall.
Party over, we snuggle into sleep
but even waking to devour stacks
of pancakes and gulp down mugs

full of cocoa, we cannot shake
that sense of something watching
from the other side, waiting for our
whispered count to rise to its end.

Learning the Line

Scab-kneed, sucking an orange popsicle,
she watches us play school under the lilac's
blue shadow, not one foot over the line.
Then Tommy issues the order—"Kick her, girls"
and one hundred Sundays of Calvary cut-outs—
even the threat of Mom's stinging switch
or August's hellfire beating down on us
as we leave that shady patch—cannot pull
me from this sin. We stalk the edges
where she stands calm as dew on grass,
slurping and waiting for what comes next.

Tommy calls her Short Bus Kim and we chirp
along. We spit when he spits, kick when
he kicks, thump bone on bone while
she holds her ground. Hot work keeping
this girl in place. Then she catches
my eye. "Want a bite?" so I lean in
to receive her gift. It is a burst of light
on my parched tongue. I swallow
and become lit up—every freckle,
bramble-scratched knees, gym shoe
swinging high on command—
"Okay, now kick her again."

Lost Claims

Mica glitters in the driveway's
red ruts, snowbush heads
bow down, brush the dust
peppering windows, tables,
every corner of the place.
"My heart's gone thick," she says,
picking burrs from Old Ted's
scruff. "The beat's off pace
and once I'm three hours dead
they'll storm this hill to take
this land." I ask her why,
claim that I don't understand.

I note the boundary line,
her trees—pin cherry,
hemlock, one suffering ash
split by lightning years ago.
"That's yours, Aunt Ruth."
Still she says "No," and smiles,
smacks the dog's coarse rump
ordering him to steer away
from prickle vines and trouble.
I argue—but I think I know
that hemlock waits to be
a stump, her house and yard
a history gone to rubble.

Pulmonary

generations of our family men
fought to breathe, resisted

those wet-lunged, squeezed
out, handed down tunes

sucking for air inside
an egg-blue back room

bony legs bound by
night soaked sheets

those grandfathers, uncles,
slept gray, blew out dreams

of riding gravity's wild
current to the still pool

springing after the gun's
cock-to-trigger-eyed blast

toward joy, chasing the kill
down Plum Knob to the creek's

root-tangled bank. Even now
he lies panting that old song

whistling out every note
carried up before the flood—

then he slumps at the bed's edge
to wait, squinting at the door,

set for that journey, long and true
as a coal barge sluicing its way

toward Ohio, or a blade
gribbling into raw pine

Preacher Nash

your Word will follow
us from that hay fever
Sunday squeezed into
a back row pew, held
against your hard wood
thrust, your voice leaking
syrup then splitting
to a river's rush
we rode gasping,
wide-eyed girl
sinners naked
in strapless pink
dresses we chose
for visiting, way too lippy
singing "Near the Cross"
next to Grandma, sucking
the color clean out of our
Starlight mints, fixing
our minds on the altar,
praying with every head
bowed, every eye closed
that we, too, might be
snatched away—saved
in the nick of time

American Girl Doll, Kit, Rides the Ohio

"You will fall in," my mother forecasted
when I clomped way too close to wet
deck rails to show my doll how to whistle
bob-white calls at men working the black-
stacked barges—how to end spit's momentum
inside the river's gulp and flow. Told Mom "No
I won't," because I knew the Anderson Ferry
buoyed me in high princess style, like no other
girl, but that day she yanked me back, jailed
me so close that I lost the mist's fish-sharp smell
inside of her hug. I stood there dreaming up
plump night-crawlers wound tight on the line,
a garfish's scissoring jaws nipping
at the current, the Little Boone taking me
on past Hebron to the far end of the world.

Mid-river and Mama got preoccupied enough
for me to leave her side, and there I squatted,
slipped up and lost that doll who once straddled
my hip, looking for adventure. She floated
along behind the boat then sank, lazy-haired,
into the green gloam. I said nothing while
her blonde strands spread to dandelion puffs,
inviting that dream blow, that wish held in
for so long, then—in one quick breath—let go.

Granny Stella Was a Chicken Chopping Mama

For my mother, Nancy, who followed

You wanting to go with me?
Gonna make my little Nan some chicken dumplings.
Get your boots on, then, and hand me that bucket.
Stay away from the banty or she will peck a mean
       hole in you.
You just stick close to my apron like a baby chick, okay?
We're getting us some dinner.
Look at you on that old ash stump perched like a pullet.
Come on down now and help.
There we go. Toss 'em some of that feed. Not too
       much—there.
Be sure you steer clear of that axe blade, girl.
I said to stick close to my apron.
Outta here, old biddy!
See? Almost got ya, didn't she?
What did I say about that? Stick close.
Well, look who's strutting his stuff now. Mister rooster's
       all full of himself today.
Toss him a good bite, too—let's give him one more happy
       minute.
Okay. You stay back for this part. Here's what you
       gotta do—
lean in close like this so he bends toward your corn
       feed, then—ha!
One hard shake real quick, just like this, then a wrist-
       snap like this and look—
he's limp as a chicken noodle in soup, see?
Don't cry, dumpling. He's gonna fill up your belly,
       believe me.
God sent him special order for our dinner table. He
       knows his place in the pot.
Now you can really help me. Hold him from rollin' off
       that stump.
There, just like that.
Keep your fingers from the axe. Back off from the neck
       or you'll be a mess.
Okay, now. One, two, three.

My Mother's Dulcimer

I hear the whisper of it
sliding from her grip,
catch that smack of wood
on concrete. Pick it up,
see the split face, a long
cut along the sound hole.

She reaches out, shaking
as if she's sick in bed
receiving the last grandbaby
in her arms. She cradles it
against her heart, gives me
a look: *I will never play
this one again.* Fingers
brush cracks stretching
past the wicked fault-line
then she strikes a chord.

My mother's dulcimer sang
like no other—bird's eye maple
faced with hummingbird
sound holes, hourglass body
droning out mixolydian tears—
those stone hard ballads
we'll all come to know.

Drone String

we all have our porch songs ready
to pull from the case, mine smelling
of red dirt flecked with mica, tasting iron
wet from Brasstown Bald Creek's current
hear the drone strumming one round
note over and over again, telling how
the old folks left the Isles, scrabbled up
dinner hollering for the Whippoorwill
the Blackest Crow, Coo Coo crooning
over Pretty Saro gone forever from home
a place now grounded in the mountain's
shadow—I rise from the dark creek
water baptized by wailing harmonies
sung in a way to cut my ears so I will
not forget to come from this dulcimer
shaped like an hour glass, strumming out
tunes blown from the grove, from the grave
my mother's dulcimer sings of time gone by
so easy to play folks say but they don't hear
like I do—the whine of a northbound train
or shouts from a boy felling logs of white pine
onto Tennessee ground, melody shaped
then plucked robin's egg blue, the tones
of four generations steered straight
by aunts and grandmothers who set their jaw
lines sharper than the Cherokee ridges made
to climb the valley of shadows, chanting
finding no rest between slow-sounded notes
my mother's callused fingers hold down
the strings of this good old song I sing

II. Who'll Sing the Song?

Tellico Days

Dad blinked, came up
from the gray place
and walked on home

to himself, telling us all
about his Notchey Creek
school days, playing Indians

on top of Red Hill, whipping
hickory nuts to a bone-
smacking sting, spitting

melon seeds to leave
a clear enemy trail
for his brothers following,

ropes in hand. Told how
he hid in the outhouse
peeking through the moon-

hole at them, sucking in
breath. God, that stink
hit hard but if he blew his

cover, all would be lost.
We called in the nurse
to witness this miracle,

this dumbfounding return
to table talk and memory.
"Wait," then Dad raised

a bent finger. "Lost
my balance and fell in."
We all laughed, wept,

hugged. "So I gave
myself up," he said,
then said no more.

Collapse

Snake root hides the path
to three hives he named
for favorite constellations—
Orion, Cassiopeia, Andromeda.
She takes along a fat stick
for whacking her way
to the south-facing field
now overrun with webs
and bull thistle weeds. *He
loved those damned bees*,
she speaks to burnt out
blackberry canes biting
her ankles and wrists.
Should have suited up,
but the white cotton
sleeves hold his honey
and wax smell, uncapping
too much memory. She sees
the white boxes, elfin church
houses or cottages tucked
into a wild spur of meadow.

Already the bees are awake
droning a purpose, sparking
and winging toward gold—
they know the paths to take,
the mindful work to be done.
Maybe she'll be stung, no
gloves, no netting to protect
her face. She leans low
to hear the thrumming song
they make in their gathering.
He's gone. She whispers
so they will know to transmit
the psalm: *He's gone,
dear ones. He's gone.*

Child Fiddler

The first time he scratched over
the strings, his father hissed

"That's garbage, not a note,"
then whipped away the bow

and fiddle, too. Reels sparked
from his whitened grip, then

waned to airs and waltzes, spoke
language a careless boy could lose.

He swore one day to match his old
man's fire—chase after each night

with the same whiskey hard strike
of a bow—and so he held the hot

neck until his fingers burned
to a shine. He would not lose.

In two seasons they stood
side by side, hell twinning

"Soldier's Joy" while people
cheered and cried for a boy

barely old enough to spell out the names
of tunes he played. He wiped his strings

and bowed again, this scrappy son
who could spin a banshee's screech

around, beat the devil's cry into long
quivering tones to call back the lost

and send them on the path to home.
In time, he struck out to find his own

sound—became an original man,
the best around—at long last, great.

Before his father died, wheezing out
angry curses for whoever cared to listen,

he eyed his boy sleeping in a metal chair
near the hospital bed and lifted his hand

in the air to strike, or perhaps mark
a revelation He gave no words to this son

who already knew enough to unlatch
the dusty case and tune up the fiddle

so that every note could sound
a story worthy of passing on.

Twenty-One Gun Salute

Great Uncle Jack was a Tennessee red dirt grubbing,
hill loving Irish transplant who drank plenty of whiskey
in his day. Tough talking from the bar stool, rambling

ridges to dodge drafts and fists, this man's hair
turned cotton white, then his freckles faded along with
his eyesight and his thirst. He loved books on tape—

Stephen King and Dickens kept him happy
in a spring-busted recliner in the back room.
When I rode in his truck, I fretted over spider

cracks webbing the windshield, but he said "Don't
worry—I can't see the road anyway." Even
driving blind, he got where he needed to go.

Standing by his open grave at the home hill
cemetery, I jump with each rifle crack.
Seven volleys over children whining,

Grams' small sobs—cousins laughing
about his AWOL escape from the red, white and blue
blaze set by his sworn signature—old Jack

going out with a president's bang. Could be enough
blasts to raise the spirit of any boy who used to run
these tight roads wondering where the hell to go next.

Barlow Knife

I.
You hop the rails, river-sniffing
and listening to the talk of vireos
and crows, spot the carved, horse-
apple wood handle gummed by
moss and dirt, tucked under
a stand of mayapple.
The rain has stopped.
You sit on the crosstie
polishing the blade
and humming inside
a rare shade of green
set to fade in one week.
No trains in sight.

II.
Ten, maybe twelve years ago
they hauled off that Gibson
who was gut-ripped by his own
knife, surprised by the dealer's
quick reflexes—some pill-shoving
double-crossing ruiner of lives
stealing the stash and the cash,
snuff-dipping murderer jumping
the train to Portsmouth, leaving
the mess behind—a near boy, bent
as an osage branch, bleeding but
singing goodbye to sun, sky, river.

III.
He sat on the rock wall, waiting
for his line to break the flat gold
of the river, for worms to twist up
hungry catfish, even a drumhead
to take home. Something that did
not smell like sulfur or blood
on his hands. The metal tinge
of a fish—he wished for it then,

sometimes flipping open the knife
he kept inside the dresser
his grandfather carved.
Then the man came by
to make the deal.

IV.
He stands, a boy, near his grandfather's bed.
You are not there but the room smells
of camphor, dough rising, onion sets
drying in a kitchen window. Outside—
fog roping the river, a rattle of tracks.
The old man holds the knife, explaining
mumblety peg—tells him to whittle
tiny things and give them to the girls
he loves. Tells him to carry, then
pass on such gifts with care.

A Field of Crows

They rise from rushes, cutting
across the sky in a line of black
bullets. Passing, they memorize
each tree, thatched bothies, sheep
grazing the territory left behind.
Liscannor stone walls carve
puzzles in the slopes tumbled
down, falling out. In time,
the wind-smacked Burren
exhales tired ghosts, each rising
to reclaim a famine penny gone
unpaid. They sing as they sang
in living work—of birds winging,
boats sailing, thickest chains sparked
apart by blood, sweat. Bleached dolmens
keep their secrets and turf-torn bogs
hide their bones. Each sheer cliff wails
their old keenings, reminding folks that
losing repeats itself stone by stone,
acre by acre. Trace the lines of men
stooped low along the hills, hungry,
hell-bent on spontaneous flight.

Mikey

Passing through the fat end of Jellico
we whined to Dad, hungry as bears.
"You don't know that ache," he said
and remembered his cousin Mikey,
how he used to roam the back woods
for days, eating off squirrels and nettles.
We asked why anyone would choose
to do things that way, with a mom
planted by the kitchen stove dropping
biscuits, browning up enough pork
chops for an army. "Just in his nature,"
Dad answered, then got quiet for miles.
We only knew the Mikey who hunched
at the table, wet wheezing, flipping
kings and aces to beat our hands
every time. He didn't talk much.
When he died, the little house trailer
at the edge of the home place fell
to rot and honeysuckle vines, then
came the time when all that land
was clear-cut and turned over.
Leaving the fog, Dad spoke again:
"He was a strange one, a good one."

Minor Flood

Grams named her a pesky
uprising child who would
make another sorry mess
but looking out there I saw

a roiling chocolate milk bath,
a witch's cauldron spilling
poison or hot lava to chase me
into a nightmare's bleak dead

end. We lifted and cram-loaded
family possessions until the wind
whipped up another killer storm
and Gramps hollered that we'd

better make fast work then get uphill.
So I helped my father set wooden
blocks under Lazy-Boys and scoot
the hand-carved walnut floor clock

past the front room step. We rolled
up two worn throw rugs, then left
her in a crazy spell, slinging branches,
and snake-licking at roadside weeds.

We came back two weeks later,
Grandpa wheezing up the path,
bent as horse apple wood. Grams
sighing gospel tunes as she mopped

down floors. The moon rose
above the mess of dried out
plants and phlegmy plastic
twisted into rainbow knots.

I saw it glittering out there,
winking me over to root in
the rubble. 'You come back!"
Grams hollered about cotton

mouths, broken glass, germs
mutating into God knows what.
But with her still calling my name
I crossed the porch wall and leapt

over the water-worn ditch to fish
up my prize: a bent spoon, no
longer stirring a pot, unfit to
feed a family or grace a table.

Family Reunion, 1979

Some dishes on the table steam
with extra spice, secret ingredients.
"Stay away from that one," she hiss-
whispers, bending a plucked eyebrow
toward the red-haltered (*half-naked*)
high-heeled (*teeter-tottering*) cousin
once removed. "She'll sink her teeth in
just as soon as look at ya." Makes me
hungry for a little taste of something,
so I spoon in, overfilling my plate,
recalling that magical oldest girl who
held a bridle between glossy nails,
leading me far across ironweed
fields on a dapple-butted pony.

Biting down hard on a hay stem,
she taught us to sing uncut versions
of "Miss Lucy Had a Steamboat"
under God's own sky while inside
raged a kitchen table war—rapid-fire
grown-up attacks over stacks of bills
and deployed probate shares. Not
that we cared. All of us knew enough
to steer clear. We choked back tattle-
tales and staunched our own blood
with leaves pulled from the sweet gum.
We peed bubbling streams behind
the shed while this Queen showed
us how to swing our hips in a round-
about stir, going somewhere good.
She said she'd go one day—and did.

Auntie, with an elephant's memory, cuts
her food, whispering about that time *she*
came back home with nerve enough to rip
right through a family Christmas dinner,
cougar-clinging to her college boy lover
and a fifth of Jim Beam. I just nod
but want to say, who cares? Can't you

hear her laughing over there, unbridled
and prancing for all of our best soup-
stirring stories, our fastest front porch
picking? She's come home to us again.
Now, she's dancing right on the table, more
than ready to gobble up the sweetest crumbs.

JoAnne

She'd swig down diet cola, curling
tight-lipped smoke, whispering
jokes to my mother, then cackling
louder than any peahen. If we asked

for the punch lines, she would grin
and catch us in her bony arms. "You
kids," she'd whine, "always poking in
your noses, growing up so fast." This rat

of a woman held on long enough to jab
our ribs and find the soft plum breasts
we worked so hard to keep hidden.
She held no reverence for sacred

or forbidden things. Every visit
would bring us a lesson—we knew
about the jack of spades tattoo stamped
blue-black on her ass, snatches

of that wicked recurring dream
about her gynecologist, snippets
of why a gay cousin died. Our cheeks
burned when we heard what budded

inside the pink bra her daughter wore,
how their beagle in heat, that little whore,
beat the neighborhood with her tail curled
in the air. Joanne smoked and snapped

her gum when the gossip turned wild.
Mom would finally come to life, cut
her eyes right to the back screen door,
a warning to each and every child

that some table talk was not meant
to hear. We stood up and cleared out
to the yard to play, wondering what else
a woman like that might have to say.

Grandma Mary and Great-Aunt Ruth Sorting Through Old Pictures

That was a locust summer—remember how them bugs bulleted our shins when we ran down the road? We like to never got you in that dress, Mother worrying we'd be late getting to the baby's funeral. First thing you did was find the dog and get muddy paw prints all over those white ruffles, you and her both crying before we even stepped a foot into the churchyard. Should have tanned your spoiled little hide but no, she just wiped you down. Never even said boo.

Moving Out

No way she's gonna let a bunch of unwashed druggies touch her mother's mother's pie safe
or scratch up the walnut trunk her son built with his own two hands. Only a U-Haul plus
a half-dozen grandchildren will do, so Sis and I work the back bedroom, knee-deep in
shoes, plastic graveyard bouquets and Beanie Babies stuffed into milk crates for great-
grandkids to enjoy on a rainy day. We box each fuzzy critter, promising storage in
my dry basement. Good times wind through all the junk—Grandma sits down on
the trunk, saying "Junk to you, maybe, but not to me," pressing both hands to
her eyes because we've just found Grandpa's eel skin wallet with our own
young faces peeking through the creased picture flap—his Plugarshum
and Skeeterbom. Inside the quiet, we pack away questions of what
to do with the mountain of taped boxes—just stack it all
on the breezeway and sit down to a strong pot
of coffee or get this over with, loading
what's left on the idling truck
to make the final run?

Cracker Barrel Education

Grams leaves the front porch
rocker lured by horehound drops,
wants a little something sweet
to pass that hungry time waiting
for them to seat sixteen for dinner.
Three Hank tunes and a checker
game later, I see that her chair sits
empty. Nosey me, I go in there
to find her kneeling in broken
crockery and cinnamon sticks,
scattered angel pins, too—some
young clerk bent low: "Honey,
here, let me get that for you now"
and of course she's saying "No
way" and refusing to rise from
the work of righting her mess.
People stare, but no sir, she won't
even go when he asks twice, voice
maple frosted, his broom poised
near her shoulder. She pushes
the thing away—what else can
he do but mind what she says?

I reach out to brush a silver curl
back into line, pluck a stoneware
shard from her open hand.
That ridiculous boy slips me
his broom and pan. That's when
she stands up, her look saying
to take my fanny right on back
outside and wait to be called.

Watson Chapel Road

Great-Aunt Ruth's house
is robin's egg blue
and after June rains
her driveway slides
down to Watson's Creek,
currents cutting the road
into glittering ruts
slow-fired by the sun.

"One day I'll get me
a bridge," says Ruth.
County works fail
to show, but she doesn't
mind—water ebbs
in its own time.
Stranded, we watch
from the window
while the cat stalks
a fledgling wren.

At night, he pisses
up her rugs. "He's
pure meanness,"
she says. Scrappled
and matty from long
years of tomming,
this cat ruins things
then curls at her knees
to keep her bones
from aching in her sleep.

She tells about the time when
Great-Great-Grandma Vesta grew
dinner plate dahlias and people
carried them off by the dozen.
Weeds run that old garden now,
choking out peony bushes, hostas.
Great-Aunt Ruth says "Someday."
She rubs her arms and stares

hard at the cat out there
batting feathers down
with a sure claw.

Old Cheesequire

*For the man I believe to be my long-ago Great-
Grandfather, Nathan Kirkland*

"Buried right in the hillside near the old Stump Ford,"
says Great-Grandma, banging cast iron pots, shaking
out cornmeal for okra. "Nothing marking his grave
but a pink chunk of granite, so they say."

    You just have to find Old
Cheesequire, *Ni-di-ni- Gi-gi-li-ni*
    who must be your very own
copper-skinned Cherokee
grandpa, a tinker who mined
precious metal and patched
pots with bent arthritic hands,
singing his way up and down
Carolina logging roads.

"They kilt him—robbed a chief."
Great-Grandma flips snapping
pork chops, drops the biscuits,
skims pools of milk gravy,
sees your hand on the door knob
so she calls you back
says better not bother,
that land is all wild
full of hills
rotting brush
       and deep splits
       of white water.

Still you share his Blue Ridge
bones and love of silver warming
in your palm. Dinner's on but
instead you're going hunting
round the Robbinsville bend
where you're sure to find
a dizzy Carolina headache—

                    too many switchbacks
            in slanted
                    afternoon
                       s
                          u
                             n
chigger weeds smacking your shins,
cucumber snake smells and crows
cawing from the whipped pines.

Yes, you've gone and slammed
the back screen door, hollering
over your shoulder to save some
biscuits—could be a mistake
but now you're wandering
rhododendron thickets, wading
through the nettles' mean sting
right
down
into
laurel
hells—
away from the old house
with its crackling fire, away
from your damp pillow, laundry
piles and carefully chosen books.

You go, skipping stone over stone,
wet-footed and shivering down
the sun until you, too, fall to shadow,
another kitchen tale stirred to bubbling.

Sleeping with Grandma

The terrible thing didn't happen to her but to a boy she knew. She'd remember the dark wet night in the Georgia woods and say, "You hear that old wind? It takes me right back every time." We'd lie in her bed spine to spine, settled under the quilt, nearly sunk into sleep's whirlpool, until she spoke. "Always have hated that sound," and listening to her, I became that child stumbling through the inkblot night along Davenport's ridge during the worst storm, branches cracking overhead, rain ripping down—on and on, looking for home and finding the hollow tree. Stuck my head right inside that hollow tree without too much thought. I stood flint dry in that spot until lightning cracked and guillotined a sheath of bark, bringing blackness. "Yep," she'd say after a long quiet spell, "they was searching for hours before they finally found that boy, his neck clean broke, and every time I hear that moaning old wind, he comes to mind." She falls asleep in time and that boy she once knew becomes all mine. He follows and will not split from me—some nights still, he blows his name in my ear.

Going Home

In the blue farmhouse, a granddaughter bends to wipe
drool with a nubby washcloth, then cooling down bosom,
neck, bent wrists. "It's okay, Gran," she says,
unwinding the sheets from bluish swollen ankles.
It is March, high daffodil season, balmy enough
for letting in some air. No one is prepared

for this change, the fog-dimming of lamps,
confusing forms awaiting signatures, how
a smell—cottage ham and beans—ghosts
its way through an empty kitchen. "Yes,
we'll feed the cows. Yes, we'll mind your
blackberries and change the Dodge's oil.
Just don't go and worry yourself, now."

Nothing else to do but wait it out. Quiet
blooms into that rare, unrepeatable time
when Cat Stephens played on her radio,
when melon pickles boiled on the stove—
kids messing with the red-rusted pump
handle, her hollering "Don't you dare
fall in there" from the screen door.

Salem stubbed ash trays, Bicycle
cards stacked for solitaire near
a half-eaten piece of rye toast.
Coffee ringed table. Fields
ribbed with green, then
turning hoar-frosted.

Snick of a pill bottle
over the low hum
of family women
watching clocks.

III. Who'll Rock the Cradle When I'm Gone?

Forecast

When we saw dark clouds brewing wind
on a westward frontline or heard ugly
storm rumors we called the weather witch,

my mother, who cranked up her scanner's
volume to a blaring 24-hour world-wide
weather forecast, catastrophes included.

Drought, flood, blizzard, blistering heat—
every season invited us to become her children
again, accepting her small, wise doses of reason.

On 99-degree days, Smart People draw curtains
to stay cool and keep children home from soccer
training. They guzzle plenty of fluids—they exit

baseball fields with one blink of lightning.
In a three-day, creek-churning rain, they don't
drive around unless it is Absolutely Necessary.

Why tune in anywhere else? *Five inches*
of snow on the way. Maybe a full inch of ice.
I fall under her spell and prepare for every disaster,

covering the little magnolia with an old sheet,
buying extra gallons of milk, checking tire treads.
And if I forget to check in with her, she calls to see

if I'm okay, reminding me to pray for white death
and the cancellation of everything except for
all day cups of coffee at home in our pajamas.

Alum Caves Bluff

We ran the trail, ducking into laurel thickets, scaling limestone boulders, tethered, finally, by our mother's scold—*Do you want to die in this place?* At the first thunderclap, she reeled us in like catfish on the line, warning of lightning's sharp teeth. The dark sank down fast. Rain sprayed us blind. I chanted *salt peter, gun powder* with each boom, following my parents lock-step through hemlock groves. We found a red sandy outcropping of rock and tucked ourselves into the bowl beneath. *Mississippi one, Mississippi two*, seconds pooling into minutes with hikers squeezing in, creeks slickening and webbing all around us. A man fell into a fit of coughing, then rattled through his pack of Winstons. Teenagers braided each others' hair. A toddler bent a whine for more juice and got his mother's stinging slap and that noise bounced all around the rock facings. Ozone green flashes lit us up—trapped and waiting, onion-sweaty and panting in varied tempos, crouched inside whispers of "make a run for it" and "lightning isn't anything to mess with" and "it will let up soon." We held hands, the Ohio kids squeezing in code back and forth *one two three one two three* to ward off the disaster of our laughter bubbling over.

"Promise No Telling?"

She took that story right
into adulthood, decades

after catching him in the act,
lighting up a Camel inside

a cardboard box—stupid kid
brother, hair loop-de-looping

his ears, ribs a ladder climbing
all the way to his puny armpits.

Smoke curled out the open end,
cartoonish, spurring her block-

buster stunt to dive in there
and yank that little punk hard

enough to rip his KISS tee shirt
at the neck. Of course he kicked

her shinbone, then landed a kidney
punch to set it all straight. "Don't you

dare tattle," those slate-flecked eyes
drank up hot July. Dropped cigarette,

the crackle—they forgot their fight,
stood watching the box gasp out

flames then float over the browned
field. On a spit-shake they headed

for home, she already dreaming
of words smoking her white page.

Red

sundown
magma churning
pot's boiled over
to steaming
run, run now
catch you
in that calm
powder moment
before the wrong
thing is said
creeping too near
the cage you built
around your temper
solar flaring shrieks
melted ore curses
flesh clipped
slap on bone
and wet dripping
even if you swore
you'd never do
such a thing

Heads Up

They whisper about a cousin's hard luck—
that she'll never escape Monroe County

or that two-timing oxy-dealing
polecat of a man who knocked

her up, then knocked out a tooth.
I hide under the table, smelling

their coffee, pretending that I have
Great-Gram's handed-down Sight.

I can see the time when he smacks
her bottom, calling her a stuck pig,

a wiggling pork belly shame wasting
space, squatting down to clean mud

their boys tracked through the kitchen.
I hear him whispering words in the slick

tone of a dirty joke among
friends. She says nothing.

Wiping after him, she finds
a penny, flips it to heads up,

and even though they say little
more about it, I see a Beam bottle's

impossible flex—and the lucky slice
of glass bringing him to his knees.

Peyton Isn't Here Anymore

"Mom, Mrs. C looks funny now."
My daughter ponders how skinny,
how blunted or blared the gaze
depending on the day, how
her tartan below-the-knee
skirt argues with a pale peach
sweater, defying Easter fashion
altogether. Leaving the sanctuary

I tell her it takes time—
I tell her that after it
happens nothing can
ever match again.
You will never go
back there to where
your old self stirred
up every shape to a shine,
even when your boy hands
over fistfuls of February
daffodils, even when
the OB reads hard glowing
bones, healthy organs on
the inkblot ultrasound—
a next baby making its way.

"Mrs. C needs more time,"
but I don't say for what, don't
speak of that day burnt white
as an archangel's robe so perfect
for swimming—how her own
girl slipped past all eyes, falling
into a shock of water, light.

I know a woman is not
a scrap-thin cat, is not
two eyes clotted down
and bruised to shadow
despite a whole church
wrapping her in blessings.

And so we keep our hands
lain on, willing an almighty
God or a quickened little foot
to nudge her back toward
miracles and home.

On Locust Hill

We didn't expect an early shedding,
stripped branches sweeping against
travertine skies, the unmown fields
shimmering out hard blazes of light.

That morning, we watched two deer
slipping along the Old Road, bracing
for their run, thick tails turning up
when we crunched past the fork.

Evergreens bowed low, splitting
with their burden of ice. Winds
kicked up so that we ached to be
home again behind sorrow's door

but we stood vigil for you, tuning
in for laughter ghosting the paths
we shared. That cold was enough
to still our blood, splinter our bones.

Accident

They say
every accident
has its purpose—
the spilt coffee
only a second degree
burn and a chance
to show your blistering
thigh to a fellow
human being.

There's the baby toddling
right into the hearth
head smacking
unforgiving limestone:
three little stitches
then a juicy grape
Dum-Dum sucker
for the road.

Make-do car totaled out
in the rush hour bumper-bang
pile-up: no injuries, new wheels.
Sick pets retching, pissing up the rug
until the vet's kind needle eases them
down—why not let a new puppy
lick away grief?

Accident of marriage
until another hero
gallops by to whisk
her from the mess.
Accidents may even
happen to you at work—
yet the firing pink
slip is your ticket
out of daily hell.

Slip up in lust—still,
nine months will wax

a baby singing down stars
coo by coo.

These things tend
to straighten out—
even the sycamore
could be an accident
of white arms
thrust sky high,
a surprise sprung
from one tiny
little seed:
voilá! here
you see
this mighty
tree
before
            its
                    fall,
before the
lightning strike
or chainsaw
snarling tooth
over trunk.

Imagine trees, mountains, people—
first kissed by wet fog
and good luck,
standing rooted
and reaching high
for God knows
what's bound
to come: black
blast, rubble flung
to rip-root-rock
unhinging a sky
from its horizon.

Mountain gone, soldier fallen,
forest torn, creek churned to silt,
cup tipped
the water spilt—

this, our purpose.

Looking for Treasure

Two hours before noon
she told them to get outside
from under her feet and find
some leprechauns or snipes—
go fixate on the springtime
instead of Nickelodeon.
She sat in the laptop's blue
glow, clicking keys, cutting
and pasting on a deadline,
them hollering from the woods'
edge for her to please come see.
She reworked the lousy sentence
twice, unmoved by their loud
whoops of joy or her own
ache for mishmash
mud pies, fingertips
stained walnut yellow,
a sudden flash of crocus.

They tracked in to show her
the surprise—a bird's nest
cradling three corpse blue
eggs, a lucky find tucked in
the fork of the linden tree
where she'd once told them
they might catch an elf
or fairy if they stayed
very, very quiet and still.

Retrospect

If I could, I'd go
back to those times—
swing away morning hours
eating juiced-up
home-grown peaches
and learn to play
our great uncle's mandolin
like nobody's business.

I would sing in grocery aisles
and chilly waiting rooms,
sing and pick purple clover
in our magic field. I would
wear the crown, the bracelet,
the necklace and never mind
who might see me.

When my dress dripped
creek water from
the pretend baptism
and you got the switch
for being preacher, I'd
step up—take my licks, too.

We'd ride out the years,
never giving up Yahtzee
or tree forts or bicycles.

I'd miss the appointment,
cross the bridge—swap
unforgettable books,
or take up clay.
We'd throw our
pots together.

Dog Day Cicada

The web quivered so she
snapped off a green switch
to sweep it away. No, no,
I told her—just be still
and you'll see a simple
circle spun around
every living thing.

She cried. The cicada buzzed
and quarreled with the strings
jailed from the sloped bough
of the ash. Why? she asked,
eyes on the spider carrying out
its fatal task. She shuddered,
poking at the fat blackness

centered to bite, asked how
such bloodlust could ever be
right. I said, well, we all eat
to live. Claimed the ache
to be my own and hers, too:
gulps of meat and milk,
oil and coal and war.

Everywhere you look,
there's the web, I said.
How will you escape it?
She dropped her stick
into the muddy ditch,
dried her eyes. We
stood while the hard
story spun to its end—
by and by the cicada died.

Missing Dad

I sat up half the night
on my back screen porch
drinking Earl Gray and calling
out in the voice of a barred owl—
who cooks for you? Maybe
a neighbor heard me acting
up like that. But I knew no one
would call the police or think
I'd gone crazy. Very few folks
open up windows at night
to hear sounds and most don't
really have any idea what an owl
might have to say to the dark.

The Last Zucchini

July sprouts gifts of pollen-dusted
squash blooms lighting up mounds
edged with cosmos, lilies, black-eyed
Susies blinking yellow everywhere
I walk. First harvest,
I drop ten dewy flowers into
Grams' oak basket. "Edible,"
I tell my skeptical husband,
egg washing and dusting on flour.
He drops them into popping grease
with a sacrificial flair. We shake
on salt, devouring them petal
by crisp petal, celebrating
the fat center of summer.

Early August, I stagger into the kitchen
prickle-fingered, a fully loaded cornucopia
of long green bounty to dice into cubes,
shred into slaws, bake into savory Italian
casseroles. Vitamins, I think, zucchini
smoothie in hand, husband nowhere near.
I press garlic, caramelize onions into sweet
slop and pepper. I sip my wine and dine
alone on bowls of rice and veggie delight.
I watch night fall

then wake to load up bagfuls of the stuff. You know
just who your friends are and they sure as squat
don't need more zucchini. Counter space,
that rare luxury, eludes me. I'm too busy
for the farmer's market or baking bread
so everywhere I go, I leave my oblong
calling cards for perfect strangers to find—
people who visit county libraries and doctor's
offices appreciate home grown vegetables, yes?
September rain glazes a waxy skin peeking
through brown-tinged leaves. Could be now
that more equals less, so leaving the garden
I whisper guilty prayers for lower yields.

Frosty October. Steam rising from my mug,
I study vines wrapped around chicken wire,
leaves crimped into dry husks—and one
shining squash, the last big fatty waiting
to be taken up, cradled against my belly,
let into the house. I hold it high, turning
my verdant prize in early morning light.
"Edible." But I think of clean counters,
of stuffing more freezer racks with green.
So far past bloom time, with not one soul
around, I pull back my arm and fling.

Why I Unhung the Full-Length Mirror
in the Master Bath

Linen blouses
piled at my feet
Not this one,
good God, no—
teal poet's smock
bought years ago
at a Celtic festival,
a shrunken, comic
fit on this forty-
something body.
I stood there
seeing what
I came to see.

Coon

Grandma told Abra that it didn't pay
to be too nice to it, that no matter how
cute, it would take up permanent house—
nosing into every single thing she owned,
from cat food to gardening supplies,
and make an unholy mess. The way
she got rid of hers was to beat it over
and over with a hoe until it died, and
when, in Jesus-like fashion, it resurrected
itself on her front stoop after supper,
she beat it again until the poor thing
gave up the ghost for real.

Green Burial

A green burial might be nice—
even if you must turn
hardcore activist to dodge
a nasty eco-unfriendly
finale. Your grown kids
whine about the scars
you'll cause, moldering
to mush. They won't say
they hate the plump
grubs making a home
of your bosom or your hair
winding through dirt
and dandelion roots.

But they do
really
hate it.

They want things
to be sealed up
neatly, no hint
of decay. Still,

you're Queen of them all
and if you choose to be
tangy nutrients for trees
and weeds then they must
learn to survive—you
already taught them that
people don't need silk
linings or high gloss
enamels with dependable
snap-it-shut action during
the final visitation.

Even if they can't afford
to lose themselves
inside the earth's sighs,

you will serve yourself
to worms and wild flowers,
resting happy as a baby.

Missive

Letters in the attic
spill ink promises
making up for distance—
from "Why do I love you,
Sir?" to "Just because I do."
Long blue years worked
to pull them apart, so they
stretched as taffy held
by a long sugary string.
She watched sparrows flying
South again, he, the ghost gray
rains puddling the fields.
Metal ground out the rhythm
of artillery and clock towers
as they promised to never, ever
forget the beautiful truth.
           Then
inside of one month, November,
they died calling out for one
another—him, hunkered down
in a clay-gummed fox hole,
her, choking up bloody mucous
in a grandmother's four poster
bed. Their last breaths formed
a moon's halo and the raven
black words they once traded
wisped yellow at the edges
then sparked to gold in
the scholar's trembling hand.

Larnie's Girl

For Pauletta

She remembers when Mom leaned
against the kitchen sink, dangling
a prize tomato before the bite,

her father out on the porch most
mornings, reading both newspaper
and clipped patches of sky as odd

proof of continuance—the sun rising
each day, bringing outbreaks of flu,
depression, scandal and war.

These cycles all happening alongside
long lost cats somehow finding the home
doorstep or those plucky robins nesting

each spring right on top of the house
where they once lived tucked inside
Jackson's steep bowl. In a hard pinch

of grief, an old gospel tune may come,
soothing as a friend. Even poems flared,
following dry wordless years. Her father

died, then ghosted the shelves of books
she kept; he lingered around her porch
swing when each morning unfolded to be

one more green-gold day. Mom's still holding
up precious things—a yarn doll she made
decades ago, a chunk of rose quartz, her own

broken watch, telling the aides *this girl here,
I don't rightly know her name, but she visits me
all the time. Isn't she lovely?* Even jarring red

hollyhocks that an ancestor once seeded around
the edges of a kettle bottom remain. She plants
them in all the gardens she's grown, cutting

those beauties to brighten room after room.
Petals unfurl and flutter down, familiar
scraps carried from their other homes.

This Time

That story, told again:
a steel-spined woman
living in a green land
demands the end translation—
no man will live to rip
her tight seams or strip
the laurel hell, collapsing wells
she divined inside an hour
of need. No tree, no bent weed
ever escapes her parched gaze.
So she grows into a snaking briar,
a wailing haint, a mountain
sprung right out of her own fill
to suck back blast and boulders.
She will reclaim each bit of ash leaf
and the little wet copse of birches
draped to be a shady-sighing cradle
to warblers, trembling shrews.
When he pushes in to cut
she strikes back, then packs up
her skipping stones, grottoes
and strange-spotted beetles
scuttling the felled logs. Mud
puppies flip inside her veins
and she flexes, glowing ginseng.
This, her life—the way to be
tall. *Tall*, they used to whisper
in her ear. She carries tall
inside her heart, despite her tears.
Everything in its place. Even
that ridge, her hardest bone,
will not be broken twice.

Aftersong

We used to pile the cases on the kitchen table,
lug all those instruments into the front room
and tune up—except for old Freddo, who never
bothered tuning that bowed psaltry—then we
kicked things off with an old time fiddle tune,
AA BB sets running slick as midnight rain.
After a round or three, we'd mosey our way
into some Carter ballads before playing
every train song we could remember.

Dad picked his Martin with his eyes closed,
tapped his foot to Joe P's washtub plunking
and my harp slurps. "Coffee's gone cold,"
someone would say, but the half-empty
cups sat there way past midnight while
our songs kept right on coming. I hear
them still—hammer on the strings,
fret squeaks coloring even the sorrow
chords, Mom's dulcimer harmonic
pinging the silent spaces of aftersong.

Some mornings, when I'm on the porch
watching the river cloud brush the banks
of the Ohio, or when I go South again
to plant my feet in North Georgia
red dirt, the music we all made together
sounds out, circling back to me from
that other time. Yes. I hear it, plain as day.

Double-Winged Dragonfly

by noon I'd cut the pond grass
low, nipped knock-out roses

piled weeds all around the place
the damp pruning shears at rest

on a speckled landscape boulder
loads of brush toted to the wood's

edge, dumping it all to compost
little pond winked bald and cold

no movement, save for the flutter
of a double-winged dragonfly

posing on a dead coneflower's head
"You are my most beautiful gift," I spoke

silly in my greening gloves and Crocs—
as if my praise could turn around a season

Acknowledgments (continued)

We thank the following publications where some of these poems first appeared:

"Woman, Creek Walking," *Pine Mountain Sand & Gravel: The Dead.* Issue 18, Wind Publications, 2015; "Dog Day Cicada," "Lost Claims," "A Field of Crows," "Accident," and "This Time," published in "Words For a Better World: Sherry Stanforth, Literary Artist." *AEQAI—Art for a Better World.* October, 2013; "Woman, Creek Walking," "Accident," "Dog Day Cicada," "Lost Claims," "A Field of Crows," "This Time" and "On Locust Hill" published in various editions of *For A Better World: Poems and Drawings on Peace and Justice by Greater Cincinnati Artists.* Saad Ghosn, publisher; "Drone String," *Now & Then: The Appalachian Magazine—Music in Appalachia.* Issue 29. Winter, 2014; "This Time," *Pine Mountain Sand & Gravel— The Mountains Have Come Closer.* Issue 15, Wind Publications, 2012. "Lost Claims," *Still: The Journal.* Issue 7. Fall, 2011. "Great-Grandma's Crow Lament," *Motif 3: All the Livelong Day, An Anthology of Writings about Work.* MOTES Books, 2011. "App, Too," *Anthology of Appalachian Writers—Silas House Volume II.* Appalachian Heritage Writers Project, 2010; "American Girl Doll, Kit, Rides the Ohio," *Waypoints*, Issue 1, January 2015.

Sherry Cook Stanforth

Sherry Cook Stanforth, a native of Clermont County, Ohio, grew up in a circle of traditional Appalachian musicians who played dulcimers, guitars, fiddles, banjos and mandolins late into the night. Her singing, flute, tin whistle and harmonica styles were inspired by these old time jammers of her childhood. Over the years, she has performed regionally with Sunset Dawn and Tellico, a three-generation family band named for her father's Tellico Plains Cherokee ancestry. "Of all the venues I play, the Fraley Festival of Traditional Music at Carter Caves, Kentucky, and my own back porch overlooking the Ohio River bring the most joy." Two of her recordings, *From One Time to Another* and *Stone Soup* (Madison Park Productions), feature a mix of traditional Appalachian songs and original ballads. She also has recorded an original folk rock collection, *It's Only September* (Carver Studio).

As founder and director of Thomas More College's Creative Writing Vision Program, Sherry promotes regional authors, providing high-energy, interactive literary arts events for underserved populations in the Cincinnati/Northern Kentucky community. She teaches fiction, poetry, environmental and ethnic literatures, and folklore, and often collaborates with TMC students to provide school and public events that blend creative writing with music and the natural world. Currently, she serves as co-editor for *Pine Mountain Sand & Gravel*, the literary journal of the Southern Appalachian Writers Cooperative, and as faculty advisor for *Words*, the campus literary magazine.

Drone String is her first full poetry collection, with previous work appearing in various journals, anthologies, and NCTE books. She enjoys keeping bees, hiking mountains, and studying native plants. With her husband, David, she raises four children, two trusty hound dogs and a garden.

APPALACHIA WRITING SERIES

Done String: Poems
by Sherry Cook Stanforth 92 pgs. $16
Voices from the Appalachian Coalfields
by Mike Yarrow and Ruth Yarrow,
Photos by Douglas Yarrow, 152 pgs. $17
Sky Under the Roof: Poems
by Hilda Downer, 126 pgs. $16
Green-Silver and Silent: Poems
by Marc Harshman, 90 pgs. $16
The Homegoing: A Novel by Michael Olin-Hitt, 180 pgs. $18
She Who Is Like a Mare: Poems of Mary Breckinridge
and the Frontier Nursing Service
by Karen Kotrba, 96 pgs. $16
Smoke: Poems by Jeanne Bryner 96 pgs. $16
Broken Collar: A Novel by Ron Mitchell, 234 pgs. $18
The Pattern Maker's Daughter: Poems
by Sandee Gertz Umbach, 90 pages $16
The Free Farm: A Novel by Larry Smith, 306 pgs. $18
Sinners of Sanction County: Stories
by Charles Dodd White, 160 pgs. $17
Learning How: Stories, Yarns & Tales
by Richard Hague, 216 pgs. $18
The Long River Home: A Novel
by Larry Smith, 230 pgs. cloth $22; paper $16
Eclipse: Stories by Jeanne Bryner 150 pgs. $16

APPALACHIAN ANTHOLOGIES

Appalachia Now: Short Stories of Contemporary Appalachia
Eds. Charles Dodd White and Larry Smith 160 pgs. $18
Degrees of Elevation: Short Stories of
Contemporary Appalachia
Eds. Charles Dodd White and Page Seay 186 pgs. $18
Bottom Dog Press, Inc.
P.O. Box 425 /Huron, Ohio 44839
http://smithdocs.net

CPSIA information can be obtained
at www.ICGtesting.com
Printed in the USA
LVOW03s0607190717
541482LV00001B/78/P